THE SILENT SCREAM

TERRY DEARY

HUTCHINSON

London Melbourne Sydney Auckland Johannesburg

Hutchinson & Co. (Publishers) Ltd

An imprint of the Hutchinson Publishing Group

17–21 Conway Street, London W1P 6JD

Hutchinson Group (Australia) Pty Ltd
30–32 Cremorne Street, Richmond South, Victoria 3121
PO Box 151, Broadway, New South Wales 2007

Hutchinson Group (NZ) Ltd
32–34 View Road, PO Box 40–086, Glenfield, Auckland 10

Hutchinson Group (SA) (Pty) Ltd
PO Box 337, Bergvlei 2012, South Africa

First published 1984
© Terry Deary 1984

Photoset in Times Roman by
Kelly Typesetting Ltd, Bradford-on-Avon, Wiltshire

Printed and bound by
Anchor Brendon Ltd, Tiptree, Essex

British Library Cataloguing in Publication Data
Deary, Terry
  The Silent Scream
  1. Readers—1950–
  I. Title   II. Series
  428.6   PE1121
ISBN 0 09 154641 9

Other titles in the *Aces* series

Family Tree   Angela Griffiths
Ellen's Week   Sue Wright
Long Gone Lil   Angela Griffiths
The Chaplin Story   Madeline Sotheby
Bold as Brass   Jan Mark

THE SILENT SCREAM

1

He woke from a dream of a wide-eyed girl who screamed silently. He opened his eyes slowly. He could not remember where he was.

He closed his eyes, sure that he would remember in a moment. If you try too hard your memory can get stubborn. The face of the screaming girl drifted across the blank screen of his mind. 'If I can't remember where I am, perhaps I can remember the dream.' He tried to call back the face of the girl but it twisted and slipped away like an eel through wet fingers.

She had large, green eyes. Golden-brown hair.

And she was screaming.

Why? He was not sure, but . . . but he felt she was screaming at him.

Then the face was gone, the dream faded and he was wide awake. The dreamer opened his eyes again. 'Where am I?' he said aloud. His voice came back at him from the low stone ceiling. The voice croaked a little; his mouth was dry and tasted stale as if he had slept for a week.

The Silent Scream

He shook his head to clear it. It hurt – a dull pain as if his brain was loose in his skull. His eyes were sore. His body ached as he raised himself on to one elbow and looked around.

The room was large and low. Apart from the bed and a cupboard at the end, the room was bare. No carpet, just a bedside rug. No wallpaper. Not even any plaster; just bare bricks and the stone ceiling.

The bed was pushed against the wall at the end of the room. At the far end, at the top of the wall, was a small barred window; the only light in the room came through that. Clear light from a blue sky; but the light filtered through ragged grass. Grass? At a window above head height?

A cellar! That was it . . . he was in a cellar!

That explained the rough wooden stairway that rose from under the window to a heavy oak door high in the right hand wall. The only other door in the cellar was on his left. A simple plywood door, unpainted.

Where did that door lead to? He couldn't remember. But he could find out. He swung his feet over the side of the bed and stood up. For several moments he swayed giddily, his head swimming, his legs weak. He shuffled forward and felt his feet tingle as they slid off the rug on to the cold stone flagstones. His feet were bare.

Looking back at the bed he could see a pair of tan slippers, each with a black sock tucked neatly inside. He bent forward too quickly to pick them up and had to clutch the bed as the dizzy sickness swept over him. He sat down carefully and put on the socks. Like the slippers they were brand new. He didn't know if they belonged to him, but they fitted perfectly.

For the first time he looked at his clothes. Denim jeans and a plain, pale blue shirt still with the creases pressed into them; brand new. Unfamiliar.

When he rose to his feet for a second time he felt stronger and walked confidently to the plywood door. It wasn't locked – there was no lock on it. It opened on to blackness. He fumbled inside the doorpost for a light switch and found one – did he know it was there? Or was it just a lucky guess?

The unshaded light bulb showed a small, square room. A miniature bathroom: wash basin with soap, towel, tooth-brush, and a plastic cup; toilet and shower. He took a long drink of cold water and realized that he needed it desperately. Then he cleaned his teeth, grateful to be rid of the sour taste.

The Silent Scream

There was no mirror above the sink . . . no mirror anywhere in the bathroom. That was annoying for some reason. Something at the back of his mind . . . what was it? He knew a mirror would help him to remember. He splashed cold water on his face and felt fresher, but still his memory refused to give up its secrets.

He tried the shower, examined every inch of the bathroom and then returned to the main room. He stood at the foot of the stairs and looked up at the door. It was heavy and old . . . but the lock was heavy and new. It was the only way out, and before he started up the stairs he knew what he would find when he reached the top.

His footsteps sounded hollowly on the rough boards. Five steps up to the door. On the third step an odd, faint noise came to his ears. A metallic rattle . . . no . . . more of a glassy, clinking sound. He looked around, confused, unable to judge where the sound was coming from. It grew louder. It was coming from his left. The wall? The window! That was it – there was someone outside the window.

From the third step he jumped up and clawed at the ledge of the high window. His slippers flailed wildly at the brick wall, pushing upwards, helping his tired arms to pull his head level with the window. As the clattering reached its loudest, his eyes rose above the ledge. He caught a glimpse of white-trousered legs and a crate, jingling full of milk bottles. Then the milkman was gone.

His fingers slipped from the ledge and he tumbled back weakly on to the stairs. He sat for a few moments to catch his breath and to think. Should he have called out for help? Would the milkman have heard him? Would he have helped him? Probably just as well he didn't cry out. He was not even sure that he was a prisoner yet.

He rose unsteadily to his feet and climbed the last two steps. The steel door handle was cold to the touch and very strong. He twisted it and pulled it gently towards him. Nothing. He pulled harder . . . and harder. He struggled, desperately. A red mist came in front of his eyes and sweat soaked his shirt as he wrestled with the door long after it was clear that his struggle was useless. Finally he punched and kicked the door in an insane frenzy till his knuckles ached. He sank exhausted on to the top step and covered his face – hot tears of rage ran through his fingers.

They had no right to lock him away.

Who were *they* anyway?

Where was he? Why was he here? He didn't

know. Then a question flashed across his mind that made him forget all the others. A question that made his blood run cold.

Who am I? What is my name? Who *am* I?

He couldn't answer. He didn't know.

2

He awoke again from a short, restless sleep . . . troubled by the same dream. This time he remembered a little more. The green-eyed girl was screaming, and then . . . and then he hit her! The girl's mouth hung open; her image stayed frozen in the air – a mask of horror hanging from invisible threads. Then the mask was spoilt by a thin red line that ran slowly from the golden hair. Swiftly, silently, she fell to the floor. He threw down the weapon and it clattered.

It was the clattering that woke him. His eyes flew open. He was in the cellar where he had woken before. He remembered battering the solid door till he was bruised and exhausted, and how then he had dragged himself down the stairs and back on to the bed.

He didn't know how long he had slept this time but he felt it wasn't long. The jangling noise that woke him wasn't the faint rattle of the milkman's crate again. No; this time he knew what the noise

The Silent Scream

was and where it came from. It was the rattle of keys in the lock.

In an instant he was wide awake, every muscle tense, as he watched the door swing open. A man entered carrying a tray. A tall, grey-haired man in a baggy grey suit; his shoulders slightly stooped, his head thrust forward as if to help his watery-blue eyes to see a little more clearly. He peered at the figure on the bed then looked over his shoulder. 'Lock the door behind me, Alison,' he said. A girl's arm reached from the shadows, pulled the door shut and locked it.

The man walked stiffly down the five stairs and crossed the stone floor without taking his eyes off his prisoner. He placed the tray on the cupboard at the foot of the bed.

'Hello, Simon! How are you feeling?' the man asked.

'Simon? – Is that my name?'

'You don't remember?' the man asked carefully.

'No. I can't remember anything.'

The man looked almost relieved. 'You are Simon Robson,' he began quickly.

'Simon Robson.' That should have stirred something in his memory . . . some familiar echo. It stirred nothing at all. 'You have been ill –

The Silent Scream

very ill,' the man was saying. He was speaking urgently, trying to persuade . . . trying just a little *too* hard. In that moment 'Simon' knew the man was lying.

'Why am I a prisoner?' he asked coldly, bluntly.

The man looked confused. 'Not a prisoner! No! You had to be kept away from other people – Simon – to prevent you spreading the disease. I am your doctor – Dr Adams.'

'If I am not a prisoner, why am I locked in?'

'Well . . . well . . . to stop you wandering out when you recovered,' the doctor replied, licking his lips rapidly.

'So I can go now?'

'No!' the doctor almost shouted. He jumped to his feet and paced about thinking furiously. 'No. We need to make some more tests . . . help you get back your strength. . . .'

'And my memory?'

The doctor dropped his eyes to the floor again – a sure sign that he was about to lie. 'Your memory may come back in time – with rest and better health.'

'And if it doesn't?'

'Ah! If your memory doesn't return then *I* will be your memory; I will tell you all about your past,' the doctor said.

The Silent Scream

'Simon' sat up straight and said carefully, 'You could tell me anything you wanted . . . I'd have to believe you.'

Dr Adams chuckled nervously. 'Why would I want to lie to you?'

'Simon' didn't know the answer to that one . . . yet. But he meant to find out. 'I want my own memory back,' he said quietly.

'Sometimes there are things that are better forgotten,' the doctor said half to himself. He sat down again on the end of the bed. 'Look, Simon . . . I had hoped I wouldn't have to tell you this till you were a little stronger, but. . . .'

'But?'

'Well . . . you have forgotten because your mind wants to forget. The illness took your family . . . mother, father, brother . . . they all died. The shock to your mind wiped out all memory of them,' the doctor said.

'So, I won't be able to ask why my family don't visit me . . . that must be handy for you!'

'Nonsense!' the doctor said, a hint of panic in his voice.

'Why don't you just admit I am being kept a prisoner here?' he asked bitterly. 'What are you up to? Kidnap? Is that it? You want a ransom for me?'

The Silent Scream

'No, no no!'

'Or is this a punishment?'

'You don't understand . . . you've been ill! I'm only trying to help you!' the doctor said desperately.

'So you'll be leaving the door open when you go?'

'I can't . . . it's for your own good,' the doctor said in a whining tone.

'Like hell!' With that 'Simon' flung himself back on to the bed. He turned to face the wall, shutting out the old man.

The doctor touched him on the shoulder and said gently. 'There is coffee in the flask and sandwiches on the tray. Eat them. You'll feel better. Alison will bring you a hot meal later.'

'Simon' heard the doctor's footsteps as he crossed the floor and began to climb the stairs. He rolled over and timed his verbal shot perfectly. 'Who is the girl with the green eyes and golden hair?'

The old man stumbled and looked round wildly. 'You remember her?'

'Yes. Who is she?'

'She . . . she's your sister . . . she was your sister,' the doctor muttered.

'You didn't mention that I had a sister.'

The Silent Scream

Dr Adams frowned, then turned to go up the rest of the stairs. A few moments after rapping on the door it was opened and he slipped out. 'Simon' lay back on the bed and thought over what he had learned from his visit – not what he had been told, but what he had sensed was true. His name was not Simon Robson, he had not been ill, he had not lost his memory through shock.

He had been drugged and, under the power of the drug, his memory had been wiped clean . . . all except the memory of the green-eyed girl. He was a prisoner. No one knew he was there. If he had friends or a family they couldn't help him.

He was on his own – he knew that. What he didn't know was *why* they were holding him.

If he waited long enough they would tell him the answer in their own time. Why should he give them that time? Slowly the blind anger washed over him again. He didn't know what their plans for him were . . . but he knew he would destroy those plans if he escaped.

He lay back to think it over.

3

He spent a long time deep in thought before it slowly dawned on him that the effort of thinking had made him hungry. The sandwiches were good and he swallowed them greedily, feeling stronger with every mouthful. He could not remember the last time he had eaten.

Simon reached for the coffee flask and poured himself a cup. It was strange how his memory was perfect in some ways yet faulty in others – he knew how to talk . . . yet he could not remember his own name; he knew what a milkman was . . . yet he didn't know how he came to be in that cellar and he knew what coffee was . . . and he knew there was something wrong with this coffee as soon as he raised it to his nose.

Drugs? Was this how they planned to keep control of his mind? Make his mind so dazed with drugged coffee that he couldn't tell they were lying? Was that how they had robbed him of his memory?

He decided the safest thing would be to refuse

The Silent Scream

their drinks; there was enough water in the cellar bathroom. The food was a problem – he had to eat what they sent and hope that it was not drugged too. But it was not a great problem . . . he would soon escape.

He swung his feet on to the floor and stood up. No dizziness now. The last drugs they had given him must have worn off. Apart from the loss of memory, his mind was sharp. He took the coffee flask to the bathroom and poured the liquid down the sink. After a quick drink of fresh, cold water he turned to leave the bathroom – then stopped.

He looked at the shower more carefully. Two pipes ran up from the floor – one hot water and one cold. At waist height the pipes ran into a control tap. From the tap a single pipe ran up the tiled wall until it ended in a curving spray head. The spray head joined the pipe with a large nut. If it was joined then it could be separated. And, if he could separate it, then the spray head would be perfect for what he had in mind . . . escape.

He gripped the nut and tried to turn it. The eight corners of the nut bit into his hand and stung as his sweating palm slid round. He needed something to help him grip. Looking around the bathroom he saw the towel. In a moment it was wrapped round the nut and again he strained to

The Silent Scream

turn it. The towel slipped. He gripped harder, holding his breath, struggling till his face turned purple . . . but the towel slipped again.

He sank wearily against the cool white tiles, resting his forehead on them. His hand toyed with the shower tap and it sent down a sudden spurt of chill water. He jumped out of the way but was unable to save the towel from a soaking. Something clicked in his mind. Quickly he squeezed the towel till it was just damp then wrapped it tightly round the nut again.

This time the damp towel did not slip; this time it was a fair contest – his strength against the plumber who had fitted it. He placed one foot against the rim of the shower basin and pushed, throwing his whole body weight against the joint. With a slight creak the nut moved . . . ten seconds later the shower head was free.

'Perfect,' he thought, weighing it in his hand. It was steel, about the length of his forearm. He hid it under his pillow and lay back. The solid feel of it behind his head was a comfort. It was the key to his freedom.

Again he went over his plan in his head. He would have a trial run or two later. Suddenly the door rattled and swung open. A girl stood there holding a tray. Tall, large dark eyes in a pale face

The Silent Scream

framed by long dark hair. When she saw him she almost dropped the tray.

Why? He was puzzled for a moment. She must have known he was there. What had she expected? Then it came to him . . . she had expected him to be asleep! He had been right – the coffee *had* been drugged! A slow smile spread across his face. 'Hello Alison!' he said.

The tray jangled in her shaking hands as she set it down on the floor. 'Don't worry,' he thought. 'I don't plan to escape that way.' Of course he could easily reach the door, push the girl aside and rush out. But *they* weren't stupid – the people who had him prisoner must have allowed for that. If he got through the door at the top of the stairs there must be something beyond . . . more locked doors, guards, guard dogs, high walls. No. He would stick to the plan he had worked out. The girl backed out through the door. Keeping her wide eyes fixed on him. Afraid. Was he that terrible? he thought. He didn't know. He could not remember what he looked like, and he had no mirror.

Yet it felt good. The girl was afraid of him – he could see that in her face. *They* were afraid of him . . . that was why they locked him away and stole his memory. And if they were afraid of him he

The Silent Scream

must have great powers! He felt proud; proud and strong. Suddenly he laughed. It should have been a deep powerful laugh, yet somehow it came out high-pitched and slightly cackling.

The girl fled. The slam of the door echoed round his stone chamber.

Later that day he ate the food . . . but left the coffee. He rehearsed his escape plan two or three times. Then he lay back on the bed and watched the blue strip of sky turn golden pink with sunset then the deeper purple of night. The first stars were showing when the man, Dr Adams, returned. He frowned when he saw his prisoner awake.

'Don't you like coffee?' he asked.

'Not your coffee,' came the reply.

'Perhaps I can give you a tablet to help you sleep?'

'No thank you.'

The doctor sighed, picked up the empty tray and climbed the stairs. 'I will see you tomorrow. We can start your treatment.'

The prisoner smiled, a cruel, knowing smile. The doctor called for the girl to open the door then hurried out. Even the doctor was afraid of him!

He ate his food slowly, then poured away the

The Silent Scream

coffee. Instead of going back to the bed he went to the stairs and sat on the bottom step. It was hard, rough, but it would keep him awake till the time came. Moon shadows from the barred window crept around the walls. He watched them and waited and watched them . . . and fell asleep.

In his wild dreams the golden-haired girl had become the dark, wide-eyed girl. She ran from the cellar screaming. He laughed and was still laughing when he woke with a start. It was morning. It was time.

4

He took the long steel shower fitting from under his pillow and sat on the third step . . . waiting. The sky grew steadily lighter until it hurt his tired eyes to look at it. Once or twice he rose to his feet to practise his plan. Reaching up with his left hand he could just grip the sill of the window. His right hand was then free to smash the window with the shower head. Of course he didn't break the window in his practice runs – that would never do. The whole point was that the smashing glass would attract the attention he wanted.

Time seemed to slow down, even stop. Nothing happened. No sound reached the cool gloom of the cellar. He began to sweat. Panic. All his hopes were pinned on this plan. What if it didn't work? How much longer would they keep him here? Till he was totally mad? Till his memory was drugged and crushed beyond recall? He had to stop thinking of what might happen. He must *not* let it happen. His mind must be calm and ready when the sound came.

The Silent Scream

But when the sound came it still made him jump. He rose to his feet, gripped the sill and stood poised, ready to smash the window. The rattle of the milk crates grew louder . . . his hand, tense, holding the shower fitting, began to tremble. Then another noise mingled with the sound from the path outside – the jangle of keys. Someone was unlocking the door to the cellar!

The lock of the door clicked open.

The white trousers of the milkman slid into view.

He swung the steel fitting with all his strength at the window – he timed his scream 'Help! I'm a prisoner!' to coincide with the breaking window.

The shower head hit the window with a dead 'clunk' sound. The window did not break. He hit it again . . . and again . . . and again – to no effect. Armour-plated glass as solid as the iron bars.

The milkman disappeared from view, taking no notice of the faint tapping from somewhere near his feet.

Dr Adams entered the cellar.

The prisoner went on battering the window long after it had become useless. The red mist began to close around his eyes but it did not cloud his view of his enemy. He rushed up the stairs

The Silent Scream

and, before the astonished doctor could move, he struck him a vicious blow to the side of the head. Dr Adams dropped the tray on the top step before tumbling sideways to the stone floor below.

His eyes were wide open and staring, his mouth gaping as if to scream. And for just an instant the prisoner felt he had seen that image somewhere before – but before it had been a green-eyed, golden-haired girl.

The red mist cleared and fear washed over him for an instant. What had he done? Had he killed the old man? And if he had killed Dr Adams what would *they* do to him? He had to get away . . . escape now! The cellar door swung open and the dark-haired girl was staring at him, terror on her face. For some seconds she had stood frozen, but as he moved towards her she began to tug the heavy door shut. He jumped up the last step, trampling plastic plates and moist sandwiches, and tore the handle from her grasp. She turned and fled.

He followed, more slowly along a dim passage with just one door at the far end. It led into a kitchen. A large, light kitchen. The light made him blink and rub his eyes. He moved carefully to the door on his left. It opened on to a path that led to a gate on to the street.

The Silent Scream

He was free! It was so simple – so easy – he didn't believe it. But after the warmth of the cellar a bitter wind made him shiver. For some reason he turned back into the house. Warm clothes, food and money, that's what he must find before he left.

Another door from the kitchen led into a warm study. The girl had gone through there, leaving doors open in her panic. Thousands of books lined the walls and a huge, leather-topped desk took up most of the room.

A desk. There may be money in it, he thought. He moved behind the desk and laid his hand on the top drawer . . . then he stopped. A cardboard folder on top of the desk caught his eye. Printed across the front were the words: 'Case History: Robert Adams.' The name. Something about it was familiar. It stirred something deep within his sleeping memory.

He opened the folder. On top was a newspaper cutting. The headline said 'Police seek dangerous psychopath,' but he ignored the headline because he was staring at one of the two photographs below it. The photograph of the girl was in black and white . . . yet he knew that her eyes were green and her hair was golden. In the photograph she was smiling, but when he had seen her in his

The Silent Scream

dreams she had been screaming silently. 'Elaine Colman – victim,' a title said.

Next to it was a photograph of a youth with pale, staring eyes, and a thin, cruel mouth and fair, cropped hair. 'Robert Adams – attacker.' He sank slowly into the chair and read the article.

'Police are seeking the brutal attacker of pretty Elaine Colman. The girl disturbed a thief at her parents' home in Maple Road. He struck her with a poker from the fireplace before fleeing empty-handed. Detective Inspector Bruce of Medforth said, "It was a senseless attack. The thief could easily have pushed the girl aside and walked away. Instead he made a vicious, unnecessary assault. He is clearly a psychopath . . . we must catch him before he kills someone." Elaine's condition is said to be 'satisfactory' in Medforth Infirmary where she is recovering from a fractured skull. Police wish to interview Robert Adams of Surrey Avenue. It is believed his fingerprints were found on the weapon. Adams had a long record of theft and violence before he was adopted by Dr John Adams. The doctor took the youth into his family, believing that he could treat his mental condition which makes him subject to bursts of uncontrolled violence. Dr Adams, who is a leading authority in the

The Silent Scream

treatment of young offenders, was not available for comment yesterday. However, his daughter, Alison, said that they had not seen Robert since the attack and they had no idea of his whereabouts.'

The prisoner looked up from the desk . . . and found himself staring straight into the cold grey eyes of the face in the picture.

He was looking at the face of the brutal psychopath Robert Adams . . . and he was looking straight into a mirror on the wall.

5

Robert Adams stared at his reflection for a long time, trying to remember. Suddenly a slight movement over the shoulder of the reflection caught his eye. He swung round and saw the pale face of Alison staring at him from the doorway.

'It's no use attacking me. I've called the police from the hall,' she said in a small, trembling voice.

He just shook his head in a sadly-wise way.

'You may as well let me come through and see if I can help my father,' she went on.

He nodded his head. 'You're my sister,' he said in a flat voice.

Alison took a step forward. Her voice was firmer, angry. 'Step-sister,' she hissed. 'I told my father he was mad to take your case on! I was right!'

'He made me forget,' her step-brother said in the same low, flat, helpless voice.

'No. He just wanted to blank out half of your mind – the violent half. Father said you had a split

The Silent Scream

personality . . . a good half and an evil half. He said that if he wiped out the evil half then the good would emerge.' She walked forward till her face was just a hand's-breadth from his. 'Father was wrong . . . you don't have a scrap of good in your whole body. He tried to help you and you tried to kill him!'

'He held me prisoner,' Robert Adams objected weakly.

She threw back her head and laughed bitterly. 'You fool,' she snapped. Her dark eyes burned with hatred. 'He wasn't locking you *in*. He was locking the police *out*! The cellar wasn't your prison . . . it was your shelter!' Alison laughed weakly. 'And *you* broke out!'

He couldn't look at her scorn-filled eyes. He stared at his feet and muttered, 'I'll help to bring your father . . . our father . . . up here.'

The old man was breathing shallowly, but he was alive. Robert carried his guardian carefully up the five stairs and laid him on a couch while Alison brought warm water to bathe her father's head.

The prisoner was free, but he had nowhere to run to. He could remember only one home and he had returned to it.

In the cool depths of his cellar he lay on the bed

and waited for them to come and take him . . . to a real prison.

He closed his eyes.

Somewhere, deep within his head, he heard a silent scream of despair.

BROKEN WINDOWS

Broken Windows

10.21 pm. 12 November 1982

Mark Abbot was angry. So angry that he wanted to hit someone. But he was alone in the car. He punished the car instead. He kicked the pedal down to the floor. The engine screamed in third gear and the needle jumped up to seventy miles an hour.

Mark's mouth twisted savagely as he slammed the gear lever into top. He was clumsy and let out the clutch too soon. With a screech and a clatter the gears crashed into place doing untold damage.

Mark didn't care. After all, it was not his car. He had stolen it earlier in the evening, hoping to have a good night out.

Some night out.

It had started well enough. The car was smart and powerful. An MGB sports. One of the best he'd ever stolen . . . and one of the easiest. Door open, keys in the ignition. Some people never learned.

The evening seemed to get better as it went along. Out into the countryside, to that high-class pub 'The Jolly Huntsman'. A lucky choice. Some of the old gang were there – the ones he had hung around with before his last spell in prison. Then it

Broken Windows

was, 'Have a drink, Mark,' and 'Great to see you, Mark,' and 'We were just planning a little job – need a good wheels man – fancy it, Mark?'

He was back. He was home.

All he needed to make his joy complete was a nice girl to hang on his arm. When he met Sara he couldn't believe his luck.

Sara. She was real class, not like the girls in the streets where Mark came from. The drab, brown, stinking slums at the 'bad' end of the town. Real class. With her perfect clothes and her expensive perfume, Sara seemed too good for him.

Mark was known for being brash and cocky – but next to Sara he felt awkward and shy. His coarse accent and prison hair-cut didn't help him. But Sara didn't seem to mind. After five minutes she was talking to him like an old friend. He relaxed and began to spin his web of lies.

'I'm a car dealer . . . own my own business.'

'Really! You look so young!' Sara had said, eyes big, brown, wide . . . believing.

'Twenty-three – I've always looked younger than my real age.' He was twenty.

He had looked deep into the girl's brown eyes. She was taking it all in. 'My lucky night,' he thought. 'Take her home. Make a date. Hang around with her for a while and maybe some of

Broken Windows

that class will rub off on to me. That's all I need to get into the big time. A bit of that class.'

But it hadn't worked out like that. It hadn't worked out like that at all. And he was furious.

He kicked the pedal again and the car surged forward into the bitter black night.

'Forget it,' he told himself. 'Forget it.'

To help him forget he snapped the radio on. There were stereo speakers set in the doors. Good car this.

A record was playing. He turned up the volume to drown the slapping sound of the canvas roof and the rushing of the wheels. To try and drown his thoughts.

He wasn't really listening to the words – it was just a noise. But one line from the song forced its way into his mind. It was a sad country song. The singer cried, ' – and I'd trade all my tomorrows for a single yesterday – '

Mark thought about it. 'Trade all my tomorrows . . . give up my entire future . . . for a single yesterday . . . for the chance to relive the past.'

'I would, too,' he muttered to himself. He gripped the steering fiercely, his knuckles gleaming in the moonlight. 'If only I had my time again. . . .'

Broken Windows

That was all he wished. To go back in time, to relive the past but knowing what he knew now. What he had found out tonight from Sara.

Mark's dream was about to come true. He was rushing towards that dream at seventy miles an hour.

The needle of the speedo crept round to seventy-five. The headlamps unwound a glistening golden ribbon in front of the car.

If Mark had his time again . . . that single yesterday . . . he knew the exact moment to which he would return. The moment burned in his memory like a beacon on a hill.

Ten o'clock in the morning.

21 September.

Five years ago. 1977.

10.00 am. 21 September 1977

Mark Abbot, fifteen years old, seven convictions for illegal damage, stood at the door of a cottage and knocked.

This was to be his punishment. 'Community Service', the magistrate had called it. 'Helping some old geezer clean up his house,' Mark called it. 'It's better than going to Borstal,' Mark had

Broken Windows

told his friends when they jeered at him and called him 'Mrs Mopp'.

'Much better than going to Borstal,' he thought as he stood at the door and looked at the peeling green paint. 'Maybe the old fella will have something worth nicking.'

At last the door opened and an old man looked up at Mark. The boy could see why it had taken so long for the old man to answer the door. He was in a wheelchair. The man looked pale from countless hours in hospital, but otherwise he seemed strong enough. Powerful arms gripped the chair wheels; broad shoulders held a large, bald head and a kindly face. But the legs were all wrong – withered, limp like a puppet whose strings have snapped.

'Good morning,' the old man said. 'Can I help you?' His voice was deep, rich.

'No. I've come to help you. I'm Mark Abbot,' the boy muttered.

'Ah! The lad from Community Service! Well, come along in, Mark. My name is Ellis – John Ellis,' the man said as he led the way into the house.

Mark followed, uncertain. He'd never been in a house like it. All the furniture looked so *old* . . . but not old in the sense that the broken furniture

Broken Windows

in his own house was old. This was really old – like he'd seen in pictures.

'Antique.' That was the word. That rang a bell. 'Antique.' That meant it was worth a lot of money. Mark sniffed in disgust. It was no use to him – even if he did manage to pinch some he'd never be able to sell it. Still it showed that the old boy had a bit of money. All he had to do was find it.

'This way!' Mr Ellis called and he led the way into a small living room that looked like Aladdin's cave. It was crammed with ornaments and vases and fine china, while the walls were covered with old guns and swords, paintings and bookcases. 'Reckon you could help me to keep this lot clean?' the old man asked.

'Suppose so,' Mark mumbled. 'Where do you want me to start?'

'Oh, don't start yet. Sit down and have a chat. I get lonely here during the day. It's all right in the evening – my family come and visit me then. My son – he's a doctor you know – and his wife. Some evenings it's my granddaughter; she loves it here – looking at my books and paintings. She'll be about your age. How old are you Mark?'

'Fifteen.'

'And what are you doing here?'

Broken Windows

'Why,' Mark muttered sullenly, 'the Community Service Officer said I had to – '

'No, no, no! I mean what did you do to be put in his care?' Mr Ellis asked.

'Smashed a few things up. Slashed some car tyres. Broke a few windows at school,' Mark answered.

'And why did you do that?'

'I was bored, I suppose.'

'Hmm. Well I hope you won't be bored here. I can find plenty to keep you busy. After all, the idea is to make you sorry for what you did – '

'I ain't sorry!' Mark cut in viciously.

To his surprise the old man laughed. He rolled back his large head and laughed. 'Good for you, lad,' he cried.

'What do you mean?' Mark asked. He narrowed his pale blue eyes and looked at the old man with suspicion.

'I mean *nobody* should be sorry for what they've done in the past. It's a waste of time to regret what you cannot change. Regret is just a broken window.'

'What do you mean?' Mark repeated. He didn't trust people who said 'clever' things that he didn't understand.

'Regret is like a broken window because it is

just as useless. You can't go back and un-break it – you can't repair it.'

'You can stick a new bit of glass in,' Mark said, still unsure of what the old man meant.

'But not the *same* piece of glass. *That* is gone forever!' Mr Ellis looked pleased with himself.

Mark thought about it. Clever that – 'Regret is just a broken window.' He thought about it a lot in the next five years. It became his motto. Mark Abbot did a lot of things in the next five years he might have had cause to regret – but he always remembered the old man's words that day, 21 September 1977. It must have been around 10.15 in the morning when he first heard those words.

About an hour before the old man died.

10.22 pm. 12 November 1982

Mark found a switch on the dashboard of the car. It said 'overdrive'. He flicked it down and heard the engine roar drop a tone while the speed picked up.

The white car rushed through a tunnel of trees and the speed crept up to eighty.

' – and I'd trade all my tomorrows for a single yesterday – ' the singer on the radio whined.

Of course 1977 wasn't exactly 'yesterday', but

as Mark turned back the pages of his memory, it all came back to him as clear as if it *had* been yesterday.

10.45 am. 21 September 1977

'Can I get you something to drink, Mr Ellis?' Mark had asked the old man. He had quite enjoyed chatting to the old bloke but he felt he should be doing some work. You never knew when the Community Service Officer might check up.

'Why, thank you, Mark. I wouldn't mind a cup of coffee. Everything you need is in the kitchen.'

Mark went into the neat, blue-tiled kitchen, filled the kettle and found a cup. On a shelf above his head he found a coffee jar next to an old wooden tea caddy.

'Help yourself to a cup, Mark!' Mr Ellis called from the living room.

'Thanks, but I don't like coffee,' the boy called back. He reached up and grasped the tea caddy. 'Mind if I have a cup of tea instead?'

There was silence. Then a thump as the wheelchair hit a table leg. Mark froze, tea caddy in his hand. A few moments later the old man appeared in the doorway. 'No!' he cried in a choking voice.

Broken Windows

'No tea. No tea!' His face had turned from its normal white to a sickly grey. 'I don't have any tea!'

Mark looked at the caddy in his hand. He shrugged and slid it back on the shelf. Beads of sweat stoood out on Mr Ellis's brow and he clutched at his heart as if in pain. As Mark put the caddy back he seemed to breathe a little easier. 'Antique,' he gasped with a weak attempt at a smile. 'Over a hundred years old – Chinese – don't drink tea myself.'

Mark busied himself with the coffee, and his mind buzzed. These things must really be worth a lot of money. He tried to sound casual as he fished for clues. 'Sugar, Mr Ellis?'

'No sugar. The doctor won't allow it. I've got to watch my weight. Weak heart you know.'

'All these things must be worth a bit, Mr Ellis,' Mark said stirring the coffee.

'They are, my boy.'

'You must be pretty rich, then.'

'I'm . . . comfortable.'

'You're not scared of thieves then?' the boy asked, handing over the cup.

'No. These antiques are too rare. Too easy to identify. They might steal them but they'd never be able to sell them.'

Broken Windows

That was what Mark had thought.

'What about your cash, though? Couldn't they get that?'

'They'd have a job,' the old man said with a smile. 'I keep it in my mattress, like an old miser. I sleep on it!'

Mark's hands trembled as he tried to put the coffee jar back. He had found out what he wanted to know.

The trouble with Mark was that he had no sense of humour. Life was hard in Nora Street – they didn't have much time for jokes. He had lived for fifteen years and had never really learned to laugh. So he didn't see that the old man was having a small joke. Laughing at himself – making out that he was a miser.

Mark believed the joke.

The clock showed 11.15 when he finally got into the bedroom. He had to scrub the kitchen and polish some silver first. He told Mr Ellis that he still had time to dust the house before his two hours were up . . . and he would start with the bedroom.

Mark was tingling with excitement as he slid the razor-sharp pocket knife out. He opened the blade and neatly slit the seam of the mattress.

Five minutes later the mattress was in shreds

and Mark had found nothing. He stood, staring at the ruined bed, a red mist of fury blinding his eyes.

That was when he heard the slight sound behind him. A grating sound. The rasping breathing of an old man gasping for breath. 'Mark . . . Mark . . .' he managed to say. 'What are you doing?'

The old man's mouth hung open foolishly. Mark fought a wild urge to giggle. The old man's pale, watery eyes seemed to be straining to leave their sockets. He clutched at his heart and then slowly . . . ever so slowly he toppled forward from the chair.

The doctors reckoned he was dead from the heart attack before he hit the floor.

10.23 pm. 12 November 1982

Mark trembled as he remembered. The tremor went to his foot and pushed the pedal harder. When he reached the dual carriageway on the edge of the town he was doing ninety.

It wasn't the old man's death that upset him – he had never been bothered by that. After all it wasn't his fault . . . not really. He had a weak heart. He might have died anyway. No, there

Broken Windows

were no regrets on that score. Regrets are a broken window, the old man had said. He was right. Regrets wouldn't bring old Ellis back to life.

No. What annoyed Mark were his own stupid actions after the old man fell from the chair.

He ran – mistake number one.

He should have stayed and bluffed his way out – called a doctor, acted concerned. Then he picked up a gold watch from the bedside table – mistake number two.

He still had the watch on him when the police picked him up. They knew where to look, of course. Old Ellis's granddaughter had found the old man that evening and called the police. The Community Service Officer heard about the death and mentioned Mark Abbot's visit. The police found Mark in the gang hide-out by the docks.

It wasn't a murder charge, of course. They couldn't pin that on him. But it was 'as good as murder' the judge said. And they *could* prove the theft charge. They sent him to Borstal for that. Normally he would have got off with probation as a first offender, but they wanted to punish him for the old man's death. So, it was Borstal.

Still, no regrets. He'd learned a lot inside.

Broken Windows

He was out after four years. He'd made some good contacts in Borstal, and when he came out he found plenty of work driving stolen getaway cars for local gangs, until a bit of bad luck had meant another six months 'away'.

It wasn't what he wanted. He wanted to start up a car sales business. Buying and selling second-hand to make his bread and butter – the odd 'bent' deal with a stolen car to add the jam.

But to get started he reckoned he needed at least five thousand pounds.

Five thousand pounds.

Just what Old Ellis had stashed away – but Mark hadn't known that.

Until tonight.

About an hour ago to be exact.

9.15 pm. 12 November 1982

Mark Abbot liked Sara from the moment he set eyes on her. She was a friend of Gerry's. He had introduced them.

'I haven't seen you in "The Jolly Huntsman" before,' she said.

'No,' he said awkwardly. 'I've been . . . away.'

He was praying she wouldn't ask him where. He didn't really want to tell her that it was prison.

'Where?' she asked.

'Abroad,' he lied. 'Business.'

'You're in business!' She looked impressed.

'I'm a car dealer . . . own my own business.'

'Really! You look so young!'

'Twenty-three – I've always looked younger than my age.'

And so it went on. The others drifted off into their own groups and Mark found himself alone with Sara in a quiet corner of the pub.

An hour drifted by but Mark scarcely noticed the time. All he could think of was Sara. How he could plan a future with her . . . and how he could invent a past, a past that didn't include four and a half years behind bars.

Mark's mind was racing with ideas while Sara chatted happily about her family – 'Daddy's a surgeon you know' – her school days, and her tastes in everything from clothes to pop music.

Mark wasn't really listening – he was building up a picture of his 'past' life which included a spell on a remote Scottish Island; that would explain why he was a bit out of touch with modern music.

It was only when she came out with that curious phrase that he awoke from his half-dream with a jolt. 'What did you say?' he snapped suddenly.

Sara looked a little shocked but she shrugged.

Broken Windows

'I said I was sorry to have missed that concert – '

'No. After that. What did you say?'

'I said there was no point regretting it. My grandfather always used to say "Regrets are just a broken window". It means – '

'I know what it means,' Mark said hoarsely. He took a quick swallow of his vodka and breathed slowly to control the tremble in his voice. 'Sorry. Sorry,' he muttered with a forced smile, 'It's just that it's an odd thing to say. Your grandfather . . . I . . . I think I may have known him.'

'What? Grandpa Ellis? Oh, I doubt it. You'd had been on the Isle of Skye when he died. He was murdered, you know,' she said.

'No!' Mark cried. He wanted to scream, 'It wasn't *murder*! I kept telling them, it wasn't murder.' Instead he managed to stammer, 'No . . . no. You don't say. How horrible.'

'It was for me,' Sara said looking at the table with troubled eyes. 'You see . . . I found the body.'

The girl shivered. Suddenly Mark felt some pity for her. 'Look you needn't talk about it if you don't want. . . .'

'Oh, it's all right. It doesn't bother me so much now. It was over four years ago. . . .'

Broken Windows

Mark had to stop himself from cutting in with 'Five years and two months.'

'It was all so pointless,' Sara was saying. 'The thief did it for a gold watch. The watch was only worth a hundred pounds or so.'

'That's a lot of money to some people,' Mark said.

'Yes, but it was nothing to what the thief could have had,' the girl said, 'If only he'd known where to look.'

'Oh?' Mark managed to say. His mouth was strangely dry.

'Yes. You see, Grandpa had over five thousand pounds in cash in the house. We told him it was foolish to keep that much –'

'Where?'

'Pardon?'

'Where did he keep all that money?' the boy managed to say.

'You'll never believe this . . . he kept it in the kitchen. In a tea caddy!'

Mark felt faint. The girl at the other side of the table drifted in and out of focus. She was frowning. 'Mark! Mark. Are you feeling all right?'

'Yes . . . it's a bit stuffy in here,' he managed to gasp. He looked into his glass for support. It was

Broken Windows

empty. 'Need another drink,' he said dragging himself to his feet.

'Don't you think you've had enough?' Sara asked.

'No . . . need another drink,' he muttered and swayed away from the table.

Images flashed in front of his eyes. The image of a tea caddy. It was in his hand. Five thousand pounds. The memory of an old man's voice, 'No! No tea. No tea! I don't have any tea!' But Mark had the caddy in his hand . . . it was too *heavy* for an empty caddy! He should have known. He should have guessed!

Mark reached the bar and gripped the edge for support. He felt a slap on the shoulder and turned round, wild-eyed, to see Gerry grinning at him. 'Come up for air at last, have you? It's quarter-past ten, nearly last orders, and it's your round, Abbot me old son!'

'Abbot!' Sara said. She had followed Mark to the bar and was standing behind Gerry.

'That's right, Sara love. You two have been sitting together for an hour like a couple of real little love-birds . . . you mean to tell me you don't know each other's surnames yet? Sara Ellis . . . allow me to introduce Mark Abbot!' he said with a laugh.

Broken Windows

But Sara wasn't laughing. It was her turn to look faint as she moaned, 'But it was a boy named Mark Abbot who murdered my grandfather!'

Mark Abbot didn't wait to hear more.

He fled.

Through the crowded pub and into the car-park. It took him a while to remember which car he had arrived in. At last he found the white MGB and steadied his hand enough to fit the key.

He drove from 'The Jolly Huntsman' like a whirlwind.

10.24 pm. 12 November 1982

The car was doing a hundred miles an hour as it neared the White House roundabout.

No problem.

Just a light touch on the brake and a flick of the steering wheel – Mark had done it dozens of times before . . . but never in an MGB which tends to tail-skid.

And never when there was black ice on the road as there was that night.

When the car hit the island it was travelling sideways. It tumbled like a white dice over the green cloth of the island.

Broken Windows

He heard the tearing metal and the breaking windows.

Breaking windows.

Regrets are just a broken window, the old man had said.

Funny that. He was laughing when he blacked out.

Black-out. That was a good name for it. That's all it was at first. Blackness.

Nothing to see. No touch or taste or sound, not even any pain.

Just blackness.

But then, very slowly, it became lighter. No colour or shape, no up no down. Just greyness. But it was better than the blackness.

Then a sound. A voice. Distant but clear. Someone singing. Mark had heard those words somewhere before. What was the voice saying? ' – and I'd trade all my tomorrows for a single yesterday – '

'I would too,' he thought.

As if in answer to the thought a Voice came from the greyness, 'Then why don't you?'

Mark didn't question where the Voice came from. It came from deep inside him. The Voice was part of him . . . but a part he had never come across before. A part that was buried beneath the greedy, cunning surface that Mark Abbot showed to the world.

'What do you mean?' Mark asked.

The Voice came back to him, as fast as the speed of thought. 'Why don't you go back and try again . . .? next time you could take that island at forty miles an hour instead of ninety.'

'I can't do that!' Mark objected.

'Of course you can.'

'I can't go back in time!'

'You've never tried,' the Voice said. The voice was warm and very sure of itself. 'Oh, I agree that your body can't normally go back in time. But the shock of that accident has freed your mind from your body. Your mind can go wherever it wants. It can join your body at any moment in time. What are dreams if they are not journeys into the past and visits into the future?'

'You mean I can relive any part of my life?' Mark asked.

'Yes.'

'Any part I want? As far back as I want to go?'

'Yes, twenty years if you wish – '

'No, no. Five will do,' Mark said eagerly.

'Are you sure you wouldn't like to think about

Broken Windows

this. You may never have this chance again – ' the Voice argued calmly.

'No. Five years. Mr Ellis's house.'

'Why not just a little further back? Why not when you broke those school windows and the trouble all started?'

'No!' Mark's anger flared. 'If I hadn't broken those windows I'd never have been sent to the old man's house . . . and I have to go there. On that day. At that time! Because this time I know where to look!'

The Voice seemed to give a sigh. 'If you're sure – '

'I'm sure. I want to go back to 21 September 1977 . . . and I want to go back to ten o'clock that morning!'

'Then go,' the Voice said. 'Then go.'

10.00 am. 21 September 1977

The grey blanket which had folded itself round Mark Abbot began to clear. It was more like frosted glass now. No. More like a soft grey mist.

And not just grey. There was blue above his head, dull green in front of him.

A green blur before his eyes. Then the blur became a shape, a rectangle.

Broken Windows

Then the rectangle was given details: a shining golden star . . . no, it was clearer now . . . that was it! A brass door knocker.

Finally the whole picture cleared like a lens being brought into focus.

It was so real he could almost reach out and touch it. He tried. He felt the cold, smooth brass beneath his fingers. He ran his fingers down the paintwork – it was rough and warm to the touch.

Mark Abbot took a deep breath. Scents from the last of the summer's flowers filled his nostrils. 'So, it's real,' he whispered.

He wanted to laugh, jump in the air, cry out, 'It's me! I'm back! This time I'll show you!'

He stopped himself, thinking 'Mustn't draw attention to myself.'

Calmly he knocked on the door. He knew it would take the old man some time to answer. Mark had all the time in the world . . . or another five years at any rate.

At last the door opened . . . as Mark knew it would. The old man said, 'Good morning, can I help you?' as Mark knew he would.

'No, I've come to help you. I'm Mark Abbot,' the boy said for the second time in his life. And why not? Carry on just like last time – until it came to making the coffee, that is.

Broken Windows

The old man chatted to Mark, just as before. Told him about his granddaughter and his son, the doctor. Then he asked about Mark's past record and made that odd remark. 'Regrets are just a broken window,' he said. 'You can't go back and un-break it.'

Mark smiled secretly to himself. 'Oh, but you can,' he thought. 'Oh yes you can!'

Then it was time to make the coffee.

'Make yourself a cup, Mark,' Mr Ellis called from the living room.

'Thank you, Mr Ellis, I will!' Mark called back cheerfully. He reached for the old wooden tea caddy. His breathing became short. He hardly dared open it.

The lid was a tight fit. He strained to pull the top off. Suddenly the top came away and the contents spilled on the floor.

Notes. Hundreds of them. Mainly green singles and blue fives.

A fortune.

Mark Abbot had never seen so much money before. Quickly he dropped to his knees and began to stuff the money into his pockets.

He had almost finished when he heard once again the sound he remembered so well. A grating sound. The rasping sound of Mr Ellis fighting for breath. 'Mark . . . Mark! What are you doing?' he managed to say before he clutched at his heart.

'No!' Mark screamed. 'It *can't* happen like that! I don't *want* it to happen like that!'

He rushed for the door but found it blocked by the wheelchair. Mr Ellis swayed forward, mouth hanging open, gasping his last breath.

Mark screamed again. 'I want to go back!' he shouted, but his voice came out like the rustle of dead leaves.

There was silence. The old man had stopped breathing. He wasn't Mr Ellis and he never had been. Mark found himself staring at a wax model. Even as he watched, the man's skin became so clear that Mark could see the blood frozen in his veins. And the blood became so clear that he could see the old man's skull grinning up at him.

Mark Abbot closed his eyes to shut out the nightmare and screamed over and over again.

When he opened his eyes again the colour was fading from his world. The blue-tiled kitchen faded to grey – grey glass just like the man in the wheelchair. He was trapped in a world of grey glass and it was closing in on him.

Mark Abbot turned and ran blindly for where he thought the back door should be. He burst through with a soundless crash and the grey glass fell all around him.

And beyond the grey wall was the black of total nothingness.

As he fell through he was swallowed by the emptiness.

Mark Abbot was dead.

5.00 am. 13 November 1982

The nurse shivered inside her starched uniform as she looked at the broken body of Mark Abbot on the bed. She had seen people die before, but this was the first time she had stood and watched while a doctor switched off the life support system.

'Was there no hope for him, doctor?' she asked.

'None.' His voice was flat, tired.

'The screen showed a flare of brain activity just before you switched off the machine –'

'It means nothing. The boy's mind was alive – in a crippled, twisted sort of way – but the body was beyond repair. That flare of brain activity was just one last dream before death.'

'Will you sign the death certificate, Dr Ellis?' the nurse asked, as she covered the face of patient A/2/8154.

Broken Windows

'Have the police found out his name yet?' the doctor asked.

'No. It wasn't his car you see. It was stolen.'

'Then he has no one to blame but himself. I've got no pity for him,' the doctor said coldly.

'And no regrets? When you turned that machine off and he died . . . you had no regrets?' the nurse asked with a shudder.

'Not one,' Dr Ellis said. He walked tiredly to the door then turned to look at the young nurse. She looked very young; one day she would understand. His voice softened a little as he tried to explain. 'I always remember something my late father used to say. He said, "Regrets are just a broken window". Useless. Goodnight.'